Dr. Priscilla Naamomo O

Can You Handle This
Dream?

Can You Handle This Dream?
Trilogy Christian Publishers
A Wholly Owned Subsidiary of Trinity Broadcasting Network
2442 Michelle Drive
Tustin, CA 92780
Copyright © 2022 by Dr. Priscilla Otubuah
Scripture quotations marked niv are taken from the Holy Bible, New International Version®, NIV®. Copyright © 1973, 1978, 1984, 2011 by Biblica, Inc.TM Used by permission of Zondervan. All rights reserved worldwide. www.zondervan.com. The "NIV" and "New International Version" are trademarks registered in the United States Patent and Trademark Office by Biblica, Inc.TM
Scripture quotations marked msg are from The Message: The Bible in Contemporary Language © 2002 by Eugene H. Peterson. All rights reserved.
Scripture quotations marked (nlt) are from the New Living Translation Bible. Copyright© Used by permission of NavPress. All rights reserved. Represented by Tyndale House Publishers, a Division of Tyndale House Ministries.
Scripture quotations marked kjv taken from The Holy Bible, King James Version. Cambridge Edition: 1769.
For information, address Trilogy Christian Publishing Rights Department, 2442 Michelle Drive, Tustin, CA 92780.
Trilogy Christian Publishing/ TBN and colophon are trademarks of Trinity Broadcasting Network.
For information about special discounts for bulk purchases, please contact Trilogy Christian Publishing.
Manufactured in the United States of America
Trilogy Disclaimer: The views and content expressed in this book are those of the author and may not necessarily reflect the views and doctrine of Trilogy Christian Publishing or the Trinity Broadcasting Network.
10 9 8 7 6 5 4 3 2 1
Library of Congress Cataloging-in-Publication Data is available.
ISBN: 978-1-68556-617-3
ISBN: 978-1-68556-618-0

Dedication

To my darling husband, Akrofi Otubuah, thank you for loving me and believing in me and, *my dreams*. I am eternally grateful to you.

Can You Handle This Dream?

Joseph's life story is heartwarming and exciting. It brings so much joy and warmth to the heart of a reader. The story elicits a sense of hope and sends good vibes to you. In essence, one can relate in one way or the other to the life of Joseph and his dreams. As human beings, we all want to feel important and valued in life. We want to be excited and happy about the big dreams and big things that God shows and reveals to us. Most times, we are quick to tell everyone the details of what God is about to do in our lives. We only see the dream and the not the process it takes for the dream to materialize.

Ask yourself, can you handle the heartbreak and pain that comes with the big dream God has given you? Do you have the stamina and capacity to handle the dream? *The glory of Joseph was in his story* and he had to go through the process in order to attain to the reality of his dreams. Joseph went to bed and God revealed big things to him. Joseph had no say in his birth order neither did he influence the love his father had for him. He did not choose the family to belong to. He simply had a dream; and the dream was too big for anyone around him to handle. Was Joseph ready to handle this dream? Dear reader, can you handle the dream God has given to you? Do you have what it takes to bring the dream to reality?

"A dream worth telling is a dream worth toiling for."

Dr. Priscilla N. Otubuah

Chapters

CHAPTER 1: IN THE PIT 11

CHAPTER 2: SOLD INTO SLAVERY 17

CHAPTER 3: A LITTLE REST? 21

CHAPTER 4: BACK IN TROUBLE, AGAIN 27

CHAPTER 5: FALSE ACCUSATION 33

CHAPTER 6: CHALLENGES AND
OPPORTUNITIES IN PRISON 37

CHAPTER 7: A GLIMPSE OF HOPE 41

CHAPTER 8: AN UNBELIEVABLE
BREAKTHROUGH 45

CHAPTER 9: PAY BACK TIME 51

CHAPTER 10: GIVING GOD THE GLORY 55

CHAPTER 1
In The Pit

Good news – you have a big dream! The dream is not an ordinary dream; it is divinely beautiful. This dream is beyond human comprehension. Joseph had a dream too – and the dream was big.

> *"And Joseph dreamed a dream, and he told it his brethren." Genesis 37:5a (KJV)*

Your dream is unique. This dream is different from all the other dreams you have ever had. You simply went to bed and God revealed all these big things that He is about to do in your life. You are so happy and you cannot keep the dream to yourself. You begin to look for the people close to you so that you can share this good news with them. But the not so good news is that, you have to go through the pit. *The starting place of your dream is in the pit.* I know this is not the kind of optimistic news you were expecting to read at the beginning of this book. Especially when you just got congratulated on a big dream.

Can You Handle This Dream?

Why are you not automatically translated from a dream land into the palace? Whenever you have a big dream, it comes with a sacrificial price tag. Joseph's brothers hated him the moment he told them about the details of his dream. Their hatred for him advanced to a higher stage when he told them about his dream again.

> *"And they hated him yet the more." Genesis 37:5b (KJV)*

Even his father (the one who loved him the most) rebuked him when Joseph recounted the intricacies of his dream to him. Over the years, I have heard preachers expound this verse in diverse ways. One school of thought believed that Joseph's father was trying to protect him and that was why he rebuked him when he told him about his dream. Others have taught that his father reproved him because it sounded inappropriate and culturally wrong that his father and the entire family would submit to him. After all, Joseph as the youngest child. Either way, he was reprimanded for telling his dream. Can you handle the dream that God has given to you? Are you ready to be chastised and told to keep quiet in your quest to make known your dream to the people you believe will hail and support you? Also, your big dream will bring great big challenges starting with the pit.

Why the pit? A pit is an empty place, it is hollow and void. A pit implies limitation because you do not

Chapter 1: In The Pit

have a way of escape; you have no room for growth and sometimes it can be suffocating. How are you expected to begin anything big in life when it seems like your resources are scarce? In fact, sometimes, you might have no resources at all. All you presently have is a big dream but you are confined to a pit. Do not lose hope. Your humble beginning is only a set up for greater things God has planned for you.

Jesus was born in the manger but he did not remain there. A man of God once said that the manager of the universe was born in a manger. The assignment on Jesus' life was too big and, *the manger was unassumingly the perfect preparatory point*. Nevertheless, He did not remain in the manger. He moved on to fulfill the assignment that God had for His life. From the manger, Jesus learned obedience and ended up on the greatest stage to save humanity.

Do not stay in the pit. You might have been thrown into the pit by no doing of yours. Remember that the pit is only a starting point for the full realization of your dream. God is a God of order and scripture cannot be broken. In the beginning, God created the entire universe from nothing.

> *"In the beginning God created the heavens and the earth. ² The earth was formless and empty, and darkness covered the deep waters. And the Spirit of God was hovering over the surface of the waters." Genesis 1:1-2 (NLT)*

Can You Handle This Dream?

Even if it looks like your life has no shape or form and it feels like you are empty and in a dark pit all by yourself, look up because the spirit of God is hovering. It is the breath of God that is keeping you alive despite the toughness of the situation. He has never left your side and that pit of limitation you find yourself in will have no option than to let you go. The environment or condition you find yourself in is only temporary. There is a saying that no condition is permanent; and the Bible vehemently alerts the believer that this too shall come to pass. Convince yourself that your situation will change by resting on the finished work of Jesus Christ.

You might have married the man or woman of your dreams, and you are so happy and excited to start the marriage journey. You have kept yourself holy and trusting God for the fruit of the womb. You continue to trust God and refuse to succumb to medical options and the negativity of men. Yet you find yourself in a dark pit and there is no sign of change on the horizon. You have become the object of mockery and shame. You have attended many baby showers and dedicated many children born to different families yet you do not have your own child yet. Do not give up! God is a rewarder and children are gifts from Him.

> *"Lo, children are an heritage of the LORD: and the fruit of the womb is his **reward**."*
> *Psalms 127:3 (KJV)*

Chapter 1: In The Pit

As a business man or woman, you might have invested so much to start a business and the business is not going according to plan. You did all the right things prior to the start of the business. You prayed to God, sat down and meticulously came up with a business plan. You sacrificed time and resources (including money) in order to give life to the business yet you find yourself in a pit. A pit of debt and frustration. The business is yet to bounce to life - there is hope even in the most hopeless situations. Job 14:7, KJV, says that: *For there is hope of a tree, if it be cut down, that it will sprout again, and that the tender branch thereof will not cease.*

Like Joseph, you probably advertised your business and told the whole world what great things and ground breaking adventures you are going to embark on. Nonetheless, you have no profits to show. It seems like you are putting so much in yet you are getting little or nothing back. Do not throw in the towel. Keep on keeping on. Defy all odds, exceed the expectations of men and rise up to the occasion. You might be in a pit but you still have a dream. Can you handle the dream? Job 8:7, KJV, says that:

Though thy beginning was small, yet thy latter end should greatly increase.

CHAPTER 2

Sold Into Slavery

Do you sometimes find yourself moving from one situation into the another? Look at another account of Joseph:

> *"Then there passed by Midianites merchantmen; and they drew and lifted up Joseph out of the pit, and sold Joseph to the Ishmaelites for twenty pieces of silver: and they brought Joseph into Egypt." Genesis 37:28 (KJV).*

As if the pit was not enough now Joseph ends up in slavery. He was taken out of the pit only to be sold by his own brothers to foreigners. For twenty pieces of silver, his brothers were willing to exchange his life for money. Life is not fair and sometimes the people you trust and look up to are the very ones who will give up on you in a blink of an eye. We are not told how the transaction took place. Did his brothers bid on a price before bringing him out of the pit or did they make a determination once they brought him out of the pit? Regardless of the terms and condition of the contract, a transaction took place on the account of a person's life.

When his brothers lifted him up from the pit, I believe Joseph would have breathed a sigh of relief as he breathed in the fresh air and could feel a sense of freedom. Little did he know that his freedom would only last for some few minutes or even seconds. What a roller coaster of emotions! In Judges 6:3 KJV, we are told that: *And so it was, when Israel had sown, that the Midianites came up, and the Amalekites, and the children of the east, even they came up against them.* Their enemies only showed up when it was time to harvest. They had the liberty to plant but were denied the pleasure of enjoying the fruits of their labor. Joseph was brought up from the pit only to be advanced to another form of bondage.

You might have suffered all your life and have not felt a sense of true happiness. People might have taken advantage of you, molested, or even abused you. The family or close friends you trusted did not have your back. You are in an emotional turmoil and it seems like there is no end to your toils. Stay in God and let Him navigate you through the many changing scenes of life. Be vigilant and know who the real enemy is. The Bible warns that: *Your enemies will be right in your own household!* Matthew 10:36 (NLT)

Close relations were quick to denounce any connection

or association with you. No man stood with you when you needed it the most. The psalmist echoed that: *Even my best friend, the one I trusted completely, the one who shared my food, has turned against me* (Psalms 41:9, KJV). How are you going to repay such back to people in the future? The vivid recollection of the pain and trauma you suffered does not automatically vanish. The psychological and physiological harm has dented your spirit, soul and body. Let the master of spirits; the holy spirit divinely deliver you from this torment.

You are a wife who is bitter about your husband. Your husband might not have treated you well since you got married. You have pretended to be happy and appeared to the entire world as having everything in order. Nevertheless, you are full of hatred and anger towards your husband. This is a stronghold of the enemy; refuse to be entangled and be bound by it. The little joy and happiness you seem to enjoy is only a fallacy. You forgive him and he only goes back to doing the same things again. The same might be true for a husband. Please keep faith alive, that dream of a good marriage is still a possibility.

While some people are going from glory to glory, it seems like you are only going from one problem to another. Joseph was out of the pit, sold to foreigners and then: *And the Midianites sold him into Egypt unto Potiphar, an officer of Pharaoh's, and captain of the guard* (Genesis 37:36, KJV). It seems like your problems keep increasing. Like Joseph, you might be going through the darkest times of your life. You are in the deep ends of things but remember that you had a big and beautiful dream. That has not changed. The God who gave you the dream is constant so He will never change. Man is the variable so we change based on our circumstances and situations. Trust the process and let God take the glory at the end of the day. You might be asking yourself; Why am I going through all these problems, challenges and setbacks? When is the dream going to come to fruition?

CHAPTER 3

A Little Rest?

In Genesis chapter 39: 2-6, KJV, we are introduced once again to Joseph but he is now in Potiphar's house:

> *²And the LORD was with Joseph, and he was a prosperous man; and he was in the house of his master the Egyptian.*
>
> *³And his master saw that the LORD was with him, and that the LORD made all that he did to prosper in his hand.*
>
> *⁴And Joseph found grace in his sight, and he served him: and he made him overseer over his house, and all that he had he put into his hand.*
>
> *⁵And it came to pass from the time that he had made him overseer in his house, and over all that he had, that the LORD blessed the Egyptian's house for Joseph's sake; and the blessing of the LORD was upon all that he had in the house, and in the field.*

Can You Handle This Dream?

⁶And he left all that he had in Joseph's hand; and he knew not ought he had, save the bread which he did eat. And Joseph was a goodly person, and well favoured.

Potiphar's house sounds better than being in the pit or the feeling of being sold into slavery. A little break from the constant challenges in life can be refreshing. Sometimes you feel like you are at a place of rest from the storms and worries of life. You may think the worst is over and you have come to a level of advancement. But remember your dream! Your present location is not your final destination.

Joseph had been through so much pain as a result of betrayal and hatred; just because he had a dream. A dream that made his family members uncomfortable. A dream that would separate him from the ordinary and bring him to the place of glory that God had destined for his life. Nevertheless, the journey has not been smooth. He was sent on an errand to deliver food to his brothers and they ended up placing him in a pit and then exchanged his freedom for money. He traveled far with the foreigners who bought him and, perhaps he had little to eat, no friends to communicate with and was reduced to less than what God had in plan for him. But the story just changed.

Joseph is in the palace and he did not get there by his own strength. We are told that the Lord was still with

Chapter 3: A Little Rest?

Joseph. But how was that possible? How could the Lord be with Joseph all this while and yet he was thrown into a pit, sold and then resold? How? Why? Yes, I know you have so many questions and you just need a simple answer. People have asked such questions as: Why me? Why is God allowing me to go through all these challenges? Where is the good and loving God that I call a father? Beloved, know that: *Many are the afflictions of the righteous: but the LORD delivereth him out of them all* (Psalms 34: 19, KJV). Your deliverer is closer than you think.

Over the years, I have seen how some people have become comfortable and complacent in their current condition. They might have toiled all their lives are now enjoying a little break of blessing. Life seems to be good right now. The sky looks clearer, there are no visible storm on the horizon. The weather forecast is not reporting any change in the norm. In fact, you might be saying to yourself that life could not be any better. Finally, you are getting the blessings you deserve. The struggle is over and today is a dawn of a new day. A new day of possibilities, a new day of greater blessings and a new day of restitution. In your opinion, nothing can be further from the truth of what you are believing and holding on to. You are prosperous and everything your hand finds to do is blessed but like Joseph, you are still in your master's house! You might have received a certain promotion but there are greater opportunities out there. Remember that the big dream God gave you can still become a reality. Your present condition might be good but there is still the best out there for you. In the book of Mark 8: 24-25, KJV, we read of an interesting account of one of Jesus's miracles:

> *²⁴ And he looked up, and said, I see men as trees, walking.*
>
> *²⁵ After that he put his hands again upon his eyes, and made him look up: and he was restored, and saw every man clearly.*

Like the blind man, some people are content with at least being able to have some degree of vision considering their past condition of total blindness; but there is more in God. After being blind for so many years, the man could have easily accepted the preliminary healing. But thanks be to God because He is the Alpha and Omega. He gives us many opportunities in life to do more and become better. He never starts something without completing it. Jesus put His hands again on the man's eyes, he looked up and then he saw clearly. You can see clearly; allow Jesus to put His hands on you one more time, look up to Him and the impossible will become a possibility. God has just started working on you. Draw deeper and closer to God. Psalms 42:7, KJV, postulates that: *Deep calleth unto deep at the noise of thy waterspouts: all thy waves and thy billows are gone over me.*

By the grace of God, Joseph obtained favor and

Chapter 3: A Little Rest?

Potiphar made him an overseer. I have seen people migrate to a foreign land and they get established by the grace of God. They begin to enjoy certain favors and unusual miracles. It seems like the blessing of God is even overtaking them. Some are able to obtain a higher degree, get better jobs and live in good neighborhoods. They can now afford the finest things in life and the pain, shame and struggles in their past becomes irrelevant or a mirage.

Dear reader, what is your current status? Where are you currently located? Are you in the palace; and I mean are you in the real palace? Are you the lead supervisor? Are you a charge nurse? Are you a medical director? Are you the chief engineer? Are you the point person that everyone comes to for directions? But was that your original dream? Is the sun, the moon and the eleven stars bowing in obeisance to you or are you still standing with them? I want to challenge you to reconsider your dream again. The dream God gave you is bigger than where you are.

I always knew that God had higher plans for me and my academic dream was to attain the highest heights in education. But the journey was not easy. Granted, I have the sweetest husband who is dedicated to my love and happiness. My parents are dedicated to my success and they all sacrificed in diverse ways to ensure that I attain my educational goal. After obtaining a Doctor of

Nursing Practice (DNP), I was so happy and I beamed with joy. I felt proud and knew I had made my family very happy.

Nevertheless, there was a deeper yearning and a desire for more. I believe my vision was still not clear. God worked in mysterious ways by connecting me with a faculty at the university who saw more in me. She encouraged me to pursue a Doctor of Philosophy in Nursing (Ph.D). Without hesitation and with the great support from my loving husband, our son and my parents, I was able to attain a Ph.D. amidst the scare of COVID-19 and the many restrictions the entire world encountered. As a firm believer in Jesus Christ, I concur with Paul: *I'm not saying that I have this all together, that I have it made. But I am well on my way, reaching out for Christ, who has so wondrously reached out for me. Friends, don't get me wrong: By no means do I count myself an expert in all of this, but I've got my eye on the goal, where God is beckoning us onward—to Jesus. I'm off and running, and I'm not turning back* Philippians 3: 12-14 (MSG).

CHAPTER 4
Back In Trouble, Again

Back in trouble again? You might be asking an essential question at a critical point in life. What happened this time? What caused the change? Who is responsible for this chaos? There is war in paradise; but how is that even possible. The peace and tranquility Joseph was enjoying was about to be interrupted. Is this a family curse? What is wrong with my bloodline? Why is anything good suddenly disappearing from my life? Remember you had a great dream that will attract great challenges. All you saw in the dream was the pomp and pageantry; you did not see the full picture. Be reminded that your glory is in your story. Check this out in Genesis 39:7-20 (KJV):

> *7 And it came to pass after these things, that his master's wife cast her eyes upon Joseph; and she said, Lie with me.*
>
> *8 But he refused, and said unto his master's*

Can You Handle This Dream?

wife, Behold, my master wotteth not what is with me in the house, and he hath committed all that he hath to my hand;

⁹ There is none greater in this house than I; neither hath he kept back anything from me but thee, because thou art his wife: how then can I do this great wickedness, and sin against God?

¹⁰ And it came to pass, as she spake to Joseph day by day, that he hearkened not unto her, to lie by her, or to be with her.

¹¹ And it came to pass about this time, that Joseph went into the house to do his business; and there was none of the men of the house there within.

¹² And she caught him by his garment, saying, Lie with me: and he left his garment in her hand, and fled, and got him out.

¹³ And it came to pass, when she saw that he had left his garment in her hand, and was fled forth,

¹⁴ That she called unto the men of her house, and spake unto them, saying, See, he hath brought in an Hebrew unto us to mock us; he came in unto me to lie with me, and I cried with a loud voice:

¹⁵ And it came to pass, when he heard that I lifted up my voice and cried, that he left his garment with me, and fled, and got him out.

Chapter 4: Back In Trouble, Again

^{16} *And she laid up his garment by her, until his lord came home.*

^{17} *And she spake unto him according to these words, saying, The Hebrew servant, which thou hast brought unto us, came in unto me to mock me:*

^{18} *And it came to pass, as I lifted up my voice and cried, that he left his garment with me, and fled out.*

^{19} *And it came to pass, when his master heard the words of his wife, which she spake unto him, saying, After this manner did thy servant to me; that his wrath was kindled.*

^{20} *And Joseph's master took him, and put him into the prison, a place where the king's prisoners were bound: and he was there in the prison.*

The enemy is crafty and Bible cautions believers to be aware of the numerous devices and means of the evil one. The enemy can use any available and yielding vessel to carry out diabolic activities including Potiphar's wife. Joseph was busy minding his business while his master's wife was busy planning his downfall. Sometimes, the enemy might not appear like an enemy. In fact, some enemies are unassuming or persons you respect. Nevertheless, that should not deter you from being humble and living a life as a true child of God. God is not a man to lie, He will stand for you when you stand for him. Potiphar's wife sat down and planned her malicious strategies – ensuring that one of her two plans would work. Do not be an ignorant believer, the enemy always has a backup plan. Think ahead and be ahead of the game. Although Joseph managed to escape from her lustful advances, she took hold of his garment and later used that as evidence against him.

As I wrote this book, I kept asking God, what was in Joseph's garment? It seemed like his brothers started hating him when they saw the garment (coat of many colors) their father made for him. His father loved him so much so that he took the time to make a garment especially for him. A garment that depicted love, affection, and dedication. It separated him from his brothers and placed a unique tag of distinction on him. A garment that his brothers stripped off him when he came close to them.

When they took his coat of many colors off from him, they then proceeded to cast him into the pit. After years of pain, abuse and shame; Joseph was now at a place of rest. Then his master's wife called him to her inner chamber only for his garment to be ironically taken away from him again. Beloved, be mindful of your environment. Protect your garment; it is your tag of distinction and favor. I hear God saying that one's garment is crucial! Your garment provides covering for you. Your garment can be connected to your destiny and

Chapter 4: Back In Trouble, Again

your zeal and diligence to protecting your destiny will set the course of your entire life. When Moses's mother realized that her child was special, look at what she did:

> *A man from the family of Levi married a Levite woman. The woman became pregnant and had a son. She saw there was something special about him and hid him. She hid him for three months. When she couldn't hide him any longer, she got a little basket-boat made of papyrus, waterproofed it with tar and pitch, and placed the child in it. Then she set it afloat in the reeds at the edge of the Nile. Exodus 2:1-3 (MSG).*

Be mindful of blind submission. Be wise and stay awake. If you do not have the grace to run like Joseph did, then do not even attempt to go near Potiphar's wife. The Bible says that she spoke to Joseph day by day until the day she got him to err. Do not give room to the devil, resist and insist. Avoid all appearance of evil; do not be caught alone in a situation that you cannot defend yourself. I know it sounds impossible to work for Potiphar and not be able to get close to Potiphar's wife. Remember it is the little foxes that destroy the vine. She started by casting her eyes on him and then she told him to sin (by sleeping with her). There are times that you have to ran away from your environment. Running is by no means endorsing abandonment, fear or negligence. Running away implies the application of wisdom and the resilience to walk away from certain conditions based on

Can You Handle This Dream?

God's leadings and your ability to discern.

How come the great dream teller was not able to tell anyone (including Potiphar) about his wife's advancements towards him? Some would argue that perhaps Joseph was not even aware that she had an interest in him. Good, but ignorance is not an excuse. The fact that you do not know that poison can kill you when you ignorantly drink it with the hope of treating a headache, does not prevent it from killing you. Be conscious and read the fine lines. Ask the right questions and then make an informed decision.

That promotion you are trusting God for might come with challenges, traps and prejudice. Can you still handle the dream? You want to work for Potiphar but can you handle his wife? Are you disciplined enough to say no to the pressures of life? Do you easily succumb to the fine things in life that are only guaranteed to last for only a short time? So, it seems like the tables got turned and Joseph is back in trouble. But that is not the end of Joseph's story. It may look like the enemy has won the battle. The fall from grace has become the talk of the town. The cycle of mockery and pain seems to have started all over again.

CHAPTER 5

False Accusation

What do you do when you are falsely accused? How do you even begin to defend yourself in the face of a lie? Who do you call for help and how do you begin to narrate your side of the story? Thus, if you are even offered the opportunity to tell your side of the story. False accusation is an old trick of the enemy. When you fall to this bait, it can suffocate your destiny and it you become lifeless. Can you imagine the number of lives and destinies that have been destroyed as a result of false accusation? And sometimes, the enemy has proofs with your fingerprints on it. This evidence might have been falsely obtained and there is no credibility to it.

> *And it came to pass, when his master heard the words of his wife, which she spake unto him, saying, After this manner did thy servant to me; that his wrath was kindled (Genesis 39:19, KJV).*

When Potiphar heard the words of his wife, he

became furious. Immediately, he threw Joseph into prison. Joseph was not offered the courtesy of telling his side of the story. What he had to say did not matter. After all, his master had proofs and his wife bitterly narrated the convincing lie to him. We are not told that there was an eye witness or an alibi to authenticate the story. Whatever good he had done for Potiphar was soon forgotten. Do not deceive yourself that everyone loves you. Sometimes, people are quick to forget all the good you have done when they hear something different about you. Watch out because *the people who hail you can nail you as well*. The heart of man is cruel and Jeremiah cautions that: *"The human heart is the most deceitful of all things, and desperately wicked. Who really knows how bad it is?* (Jeremiah 17:9, NLT)

The fact that you received a promotion is not enough reason for you to neglect God. Although the Lord was with Joseph, the enemy managed to falsely accuse him and he was thrown into prison. I have seen people meet unimaginable challenges as a result of a promotion they receive in life. In the heat of the challenging moment, they sometimes question themselves if the promotion was even worth it. Do not arm the enemy against yourself. Words are powerful and you can create a whole world of negativity and fear by the words that proceed out of your mouth. These words become barriers that can trap your destiny forever.

Chapter 5: False Accusation

Know the seasons and times. Jesus is both a lion and lamb. One of the hardest things to endure in life is when you are falsely accused. When your reputation is at stake and you are defenseless. I have seen marriages break up as a result of one partner falsely accusing the other of infidelity or some kind of unpardonable sin (by the standards of men) based on a rumor. Some close friends have become archenemies because one party falsely accused the other and there has been no success at amending the indifferences. Similarly, tribal, ethnic, and national wars have persisted for generations because of false accusation. Know when the violent must take it by force and know when to turn the other cheek in humility.

> *[38] "You have heard the law that says the punishment must match the injury: 'An eye for an eye, and a tooth for a tooth. [39] But I say, do not resist an evil person! If someone slaps you on the right cheek, offer the other cheek also (Matthew 5:38-39, NLT).*

Our God is a God of vengeance and at the right time, he will vindicate you. In fact, the Bible says that: *Seeing it is a righteous thing with God to recompense tribulation to them that trouble you* (2 Thessalonians 1:6, KJV). God himself will trouble those who trouble you. To be falsely accused is a kind of trouble that one cannot get out from by one's own strength. The stigma and embarrassment that comes with it can be so debilitating that it renders you hopeless and resentful. Beloved, check your life and ask God to help you to let go off any root of bitterness embedded in your heart as a result of being falsely accused.

Do not beat yourself up when you know within yourself that you are not at fault. Recognize that the enemy roars and seeks your destruction every day. Sometimes, it is not your fault and so there is nothing that you can do about it. Your job is to stay alert and take solace in the word of God.

> *Stay alert! Watch out for your great enemy, the devil. He prowls around like a roaring lion, looking for someone to devour (1 Peter 5:8, NLT).*

John 10:10-11, KJV

> *[10] The thief cometh not, but for to steal, and to kill, and to destroy: I am come that they might have life, and that they might have it more abundantly.*
>
> *[11] I am the good shepherd: the good shepherd giveth his life for the sheep.*

CHAPTER 6
Challenges And Opportunities In Prison

Even in prison, Joseph faced challenges but we are told that the Lord was still with him and he was put in charge of all the prisoners. A good name, they say is better than great riches. Let your good deeds follow you wherever you go. Use your God given talent wherever you find yourself. There are opportunities in every challenge you face in life. Joseph was thrown in prison but it was an opportunity in disguise. Another promotion was waiting for him. You might be going through dark times right now but do not give up. Sit back and analyze the situation. Ask God to help you realize the opportunities imbedded in your struggles. Light shines brighter in darkness.

Over the years, I have seen some people complain and murmur over everything, whether good or bad. I have seen people move from one state to another only to return back to their original state because at the end of the day, the grass was not greener on that side after all. For some people, California is too hot, others say Alaska is too cold, while others postulate that Florida is too humid and the list goes on and on. That perfect condition you are waiting and waiting on might never come at the time you anticipate it. You might be wasting precious time when all you have to do is to take advantage of the condition and make the best out of it. Joseph could have entered into prison very bitter and full of complaining and murmurings. Remember he was framed and no man stood with him. He had all the reasons to be bitter but he chose to be better.

In the early years of my nursing career, I was floated to different units in the hospital where I worked at. I was initially a pediatric registered nurse but I ended up on the adult medical surgical unit, telemetry, post- anesthesia care unit, emergency room, you name it. I became a relief charge nurse and assisted in many administrative roles. I did not understand the process and I got frustrated at some point. Little did I know that, the experiences on the different units and the managerial skills were preparing me for an exciting career later on in life where all the learned skills and experience would matter and, become profitable.

Daniel was thrown into the lion's den but the lions

became his friends. When the king came to check up on him the morning, he was still there – alive and breathing. What was meant to kill him rather gave him comfort and guidance through the night. Do not die before your time. That situation is not meant to kill you. You can arise and shine; you can do more in life. You might be in prison, again – or you might have been thrown into the lion's den. We hear what you are complaining about but what is next? The Psalmist said: *When my father and my mother forsake me, then the LORD will take me up* (Psalms 27:10, KJV). That abandonment by the people you looked up to is an opportunity for God to take you up. *When God takes you up, your elevation is secured.* They might have forsaken you but God is about to shake you up and then take you up to the next level. Trust the process.

The word of God assures us that: *In all labour there is profit: but the talk of the lips tendeth only to penury* (Proverbs 14:23, KJV). Stop talking about your situation and get to work. A person who only talks will ultimately end up in poverty but God will honor the works of the diligent hand. After all, He is the God who teaches your fingers to fight. You will enjoy the fruits of your labor. Working demands discipline and commitment; it calls for accountability and it will put a level of responsibility on you. You will get a measure of what you put in. No matter how much you praise a seed, until you put it into the ground and plant it, it will not grow and bear fruits.

Merely describing a situation in detail and not doing anything about it is not profitable. I dare you to see an opportunity in every challenge you are facing. The great inventors in our world would have never discovered or created anything if they did not first identify a need. They realized that there was a problem and they brought solutions in the form on inventions. As children of God, we carry God's creative ability. We have been called unto greater works and we cannot fail our master Jesus.

Do not stifle the gifts and potentials that God has deposited in you. A man or woman who is dedicated to a task is bound to succeed. The Bible confirms this: *Seest thou a man diligent in his business? he shall stand before kings; he shall not stand before mean men* (Proverbs 22:29, KJV). Regardless of the prison of isolation and neglect, a person's continued diligence to his or her work will produce tangible results. As a young person growing up in Ghana, West Africa I saw firsthand how my mother worked very hard to make life comfortable for me and my brothers and sisters. She would wake up in the early hours of the morning to start her business. She came home late in the evenings and had little rest. The cycle continued but God honored the works of her hands.

CHAPTER 7

A Glimpse Of Hope

After interpreting the dream for the butler and the baker, Joseph was hopeful that they would remember him once they go out. He even reminded the butler: *But when all goes well with you, remember me and show me kindness; mention me to Pharaoh and get me out of this prison* (Genesis 40: 14, NIV). How many times have you shown kindness to someone and politely reminded them to remember you when all goes well with them? Then life continues and you have this hope that one day, you will be remembered and favored.

The butler was close to the king. He served the king his drink and possibly had the advantage of talking directly to the king. Joseph was convinced that by merely mentioning him to the king, an opportunity to freedom would become a possibility. But man is quick to forget; sometimes, too quick to forget about the people who helped them to get to the place and position they currently occupy. You might have done some good deeds and gone out of your way to make someone attain a goal in life. Within days, weeks or years, such a person completely forgets about you and the promises he or she made to you becomes an illusion.

How do you keep holding on when that glimpse of hope seems to be fading away right before your eyes? One must apply caution when looking up to man for help. Even with their best intentions and promise to help you, man can simply forget. The Bible warns in Jeremiah 17:5-8, NLT:

> [5] This is what the LORD says:
> "Cursed are those who put their trust in mere humans,
> who rely on human strength
> and turn their hearts away from the LORD.
> [6] They are like stunted shrubs in the desert,
> with no hope for the future.
> They will live in the barren wilderness,
> in an uninhabited salty land.
>
> [7] "But blessed are those who trust in the LORD
> and have made the LORD their hope and confidence.
> [8] They are like trees planted along a riverbank,
> with roots that reach deep into the water.
> Such trees are not bothered by the heat
> or worried by long months of drought.
> Their leaves stay green,
> and they never stop producing fruit.

Chapter 7: A Glimpse Of Hope

Joseph asked for a favor but he did not put his trust in man. Trust implies a firm belief. When that firm belief does not become a reality, there is a tendency for one to lose hope. Dreams are shattered and foundations are destroyed in the wake of a disappointment. Relying on human strength can be very dangerous. The Bible liken such a person to one left to the dead of the heat in the desert. Lives have been destroyed as a result of failed promises. Beloved, do not hinge your hope on man; rather, look up to God who is the author and finisher of your faith. Numbers 23:19, NLT affirms that:

> *God is not a man, so he does not lie.*
> *He is not human, so he does not change his mind.*
> *Has he ever spoken and failed to act?*
> *Has he ever promised and not carried it through?*

Whatever God says, He watches over it to perform it. He performs it in such a way that one cannot help but to acknowledge that God is indeed the master mind behind it all. Even though the Butler was restored to his position, he still forgot to mention him to Pharaoh. Genesis 40:23, KJV:

> *Yet did not the chief butler remember Joseph, but forgat him.*

Man will forget about you; man will not remember all the good you have done for them especially when all goes well with them. Priorities change and you become the least on their plans. Do not hold grudges and bitterness against such persons. Choose to be better and not bitter. *Do not let the soar situations soil your soul and cause you to sin.* The Butler did not remember Joseph, he forgot about him but life continued. There is no account of Joseph cursing the Butler or starting an insurrection. He stayed in prison but his sense of hard work and diligence did not change.

CHAPTER 8
An Unbelievable Breakthrough

An unbelievable breakthrough was looming on the horizon. The tables were about to be turned and a person's negative story was about to be re written. Two years have passed since Joseph interpreted the Butler's dream and asked the favor of him. After two years of waiting, hoping and anticipating, God caused Pharaoh to have a dream that needed a higher level of interpretation. The good magicians in the land could not analyze the dream until the best was called upon. You will be discovered and you will come into the limelight.

Why now? Why did God cause Pharaoh to have this dream at such a time as this? What happened between the time that Joseph interpreted the dream for the Butler and now? Why the long silence? Didn't Pharaoh sleep and dream on other days as well? What makes this dream unique and why at such a time as this? You might find yourself asking so many questions in life and it seems like you have no answers forthcoming. You might be asking yourself; why is it taking so long for me to have that man or woman of my dreams? When am I going to graduate with that degree? When am I going to have that dream job? When am I going to experience happiness in life? And the list goes on and on. Despite your silence questioning and anticipation, you have continued in your service and love for God. Hear this: *I have not spoken in secret, in a dark place of the earth: I said not unto the seed of Jacob, Seek ye me in vain: I the LORD speak righteousness, I declare things that are right* (Isaiah 45: 19, KJV). Your service to God is not in vain. God is a rewarder and He will not withhold your deserved wages from you. Your pay day has come so get excited. God will connect you at the right time to the right people to be a blessing to you. When the right time comes, the Butler confessed: *Then spake the chief butler unto Pharaoh, saying, I do remember my faults this day* (Genesis 41:9, KJV).

Imagine what would have happened if Joseph had organized and plotted an escape from prison. Sometimes in our haste to get out of the place of discomfort, we try to form all kinds of associations and clicks/groups just to help us come out quickly. Child of God, be patient. Do not be in haste to do anything in life. Not every discomfort is for your shame, wait on God and know what to do at any moment in life. Have you sought

Chapter 8: An Unbelievable Breakthrough

the face of God in that situation? What is the spirit of God saying to you? Are you convinced to move out? In Exodus 23: 28-30, KJV the Bible says that:

> ^{28} *And I will send hornets before thee, which shall drive out the Hivite, the Canaanite, and the Hittite, from before thee.*
>
> ^{29} *I will not drive them out from before thee in one year; lest the land become desolate, and the beast of the field multiply against thee.*
>
> ^{30} *By little and little I will drive them out from before thee, until thou be increased, and inherit the land.*

God is not slow. He knows exactly what he is doing at any point in time and He got everything figured out. Once you are in the will of God, know that you are moving at the right pace and there is no need to fret. You have served God and you continue to serve Him; he has, therefore, sent the hornets before you. Nevertheless, the master planner is not driving all your enemies out at a time. And you ask the question why? God is telling you that the delay is for your own good. He does not want the beasts on the land to grow in number and fight you. God knows how much you can handle so relax in the confidence and knowing that, He has you where you are supposed to be.

When an unbelievable breakthrough is about to manifest in the life of a person, sometimes, they enemy can send weights of discouragement in the guise of fear and doubt. When caution is not taken, you might move out of the place that God has placed you and your years of waiting becomes a monument of despair. There was a time in the life of the Israelites that their leader had to remind them to take heart and rest in God: *And Moses said unto the people, Fear ye not, stand still, and see the salvation of the LORD, which he will shew to you to day: for the Egyptians whom ye have seen to day, ye shall see them again no more for ever* (Exodus 14:13, KJV).

Your breakthrough will be orchestrated by God. He will cause men in authority to become uncomfortable in the plan of your comeback and elevation. May God send men to come looking for you. In haste, they will bring you out and then set you up for your next level. Do not fight unnecessary battles and then end up frustrated in life. The same haste with which the enemy used to bring you down will be the same haste that God will cause them to bring you up for your promotion.

Look at a similar account in the Bible where Daniel was brought out in haste as commanded by the King. Daniel 2:25, KJV: *Then Arioch brought in Daniel before the king **in haste**, and said thus unto him, I have found a man of the captives of Judah, that will make known unto the king the interpretation.*

When Joseph came out of the prison, there were three significant things he did in order to be fitting to stand

Chapter 8: An Unbelievable Breakthrough

before the king. Genesis 41:14, KJV:

Then Pharaoh sent and called Joseph, and they brought him hastily out of the dungeon: and he shaved himself, and changed his raiment, and came in unto Pharaoh.

1. He shaved
2. He changed his raiment
3. He came before the King

Your gifts and talents are good but you need to follow the right order in order to be able to stand before the king. Hence, preparation is key for your next level in life. Firstly, Joseph shaved off the old image of imprisonment. Secondly, he changed his raiment of shame and thirdly, he stood before king. At salvation, Jesus shaved off our sins, shame and guilt. He then put on us His righteousness and now we are able to stand blameless before the God the father. Show gratitude to the God who has brought you thus far.

Always acknowledge God. Be careful to direct all praise to God. You might have attained all the degrees and are well qualified for that promotion, nevertheless, place God where He belongs when men begin to sing your praise. You were once in a dungeon where no one cared about you. God arranged this new phase in your life. Let people know that you are not a self-made man. You did not suddenly arrive at your current location by default. Again, Joseph the great dreamer reminds us that God is the master of his life. In Genesis 41:16, KJV: *And Joseph answered Pharaoh, saying, It is not in me: God shall give Pharaoh an answer of peace.*

Today, the dungeon boy has become the sought-out man! The stone the builders rejected and refused has become the chief cornerstone (Psalms 118:22). You are valuable; a high price was paid for your salvation. God has turned your mourning into dancing. He has been given you beauty for ashes. The weak is saying that they are strong and the poor is rich. Nations have come to Joseph and he is renowned. Genesis 41:57, KJV: *And all countries came into Egypt to Joseph for to buy corn; because that the famine was so sore in all lands.*

CHAPTER 9
Pay Back Time

The dream has materialized and Joseph is restored to his original place – the palace! (And I mean the real palace where he is now in charge). Now the people who threw him out, sold him out, gave up on him and lied about him are before him. What will you do if you were in Joseph's shoes? I know some people will be quick to call fire down from heaven to consume them. Some will hurl all kinds of insults and curses on them. Afterall, they are the perpetuators of his pain. This is payback time and the enemy is right in front of you.

Life is not fair and the temptation to play the game of the enemy as a pay back is easier to do than to look up to God and depend on the sovereignty of the all-sufficient God. This becomes more challenging when you were wounded and have scars to show. No matter how much you try to cover it up and pretend that all is well, there is always a buried and hidden pain that will continue to hunt you. The world will tell you that, it is easier said than done because the pain of their actions has left an indelible mark that cannot be simply ignored.

Be very careful because the hidden pain can turn into something else. As a dually board-certified Family Nurse Practitioner and a Psychiatric Mental Health Nurse Practitioner, I have seen and treated different kinds of patients from diverse race and background. I have seen firsthand the different kinds of medical and psychological conditions that unforgiveness and emotional pain can produce. Medical science has proven that one's general health can be drastically affected when there are high levels of stress; sustained over extended periods of time with no resolution. Further, the social determinants of health cannot be ignored in the light of holistic care. Some mental health conditions such as depression, anxiety, post-traumatic stress disorder and many others have been linked to some of the traumatic events of life. True healing begins when one learns to let go.

In Genesis 42:6, NLT we learned that: *Since Joseph was governor of all Egypt and in charge of selling grain to all the people, it was to him that his brothers came. When they arrived, they bowed before him with their faces to the ground.* Joseph was now in charge; he is the governor of the land. He is a person of influence and he is the person to go to for answers. His words become the law of the land. Now here are his brothers; the brothers who did him wrong. But the tables have

Chapter 9: Pay Back Time

turned and they are bowing before him in his presence. They could not recognize him because of the dramatic change and elevation in Joseph's life. When God blesses you, your enemies will come and bow to you.

When you are tempted to pay back evil to the people who have done you wrong, take some time and reflect on these scriptures:

Leviticus 19:18, KJV:

> *Thou shalt not avenge, nor bear any grudge against the children of thy people, but thou shalt love thy neighbour as thyself: I am the LORD.*

Deuteronomy 32:35, KJV:

> *To me belongeth vengeance and recompence; their foot shall slide in due time: for the day of their calamity is at hand, and the things that shall come upon them make haste.*

Psalms 94:1-2, KJV

> *¹O Lord God, to whom vengeance belongeth; O God, to whom vengeance belongeth, shew thyself.*
>
> *² Lift up thyself, thou judge of the earth: render a reward to the proud.*

Proverbs 20:22, KJV

> *Say not thou, I will recompense evil; but wait on the LORD, and he shall save thee.*

Can You Handle This Dream?

Luke 6:27-28, KJV

27 But I say unto you which hear, Love your enemies, do good to them which hate you,

28 Bless them that curse you, and pray for them which despitefully use you.

CHAPTER 10

Giving God The Glory

Do not give up! Your story will end in praise. Kings will come to your rising so arise and shine. Harvest time is here; it is time for the dawning of a new day. A new day of possibilities and open doors. The storm has passed and the clouds have cleared. The sun is out and the green leaves are blooming with life. You have endured to the end and deliverance has come. Your Savior and King is seated in majesty waiting for His praise. Psalms 65: 1, KJV: *Praise waiteth for thee, O God, in Zion: and unto thee shall the vow be performed.* Go ahead and give him the glory and honor due His name. *A recollection of the goodness of God will catapult you into turbulent praise and worship.* A realm of worship and adoration worthy of the King of kings and the Lord of lords.

We serve a God who is too big to fail. He is interested in every detail of your life. In the end, what was meant for evil will turn out for your good. What was planned to kill you will only make you better and you will not be able to contain it but to give all the glory back to God. Genesis 50:20, KJV: *But as for you, ye thought evil against me; but God meant it unto good, to bring to pass, as it is this day, to save much people alive.* Again, I want to assure you that there is glory in your story. Even when you do not see it, God has been behind the scenes from day one. Although it seemed like evil prevailed, that cycle has been truncated. The King of glory, the Lord God strong in battle has prevailed. Give Him the honor due his name (Psalms 29:2).

There are depths in God and your approach to praising God will determine your elevation in life. Joseph did not end there; he went on to become a blessing to his brothers' children and their generation. He quickly realized that the goodness of God upon his life was not meant for only him. Earlier, he told his brothers that his trials, temptations and tribulations were platforms for the happiness and generational blessings of many people. (Genesis 50: 21-23, KJV)

> [21] *Now therefore fear ye not: I will nourish you, and your little ones. And he comforted them, and spake kindly unto them.*
>
> [22] *And Joseph dwelt in Egypt, he, and his father's house: and Joseph lived an hundred and ten years.*

Chapter 10: Giving God The Glory

²³ And Joseph saw Ephraim's children of the third generation: the children also of Machir the son of Manasseh were brought up upon Joseph's knees.

Dear reader, show some kindness and go the extra mile for the comfort and, joy of others. It will only abound to your account. *Kindness is linked to longevity.* Speak positivity to the naysayers and haters around you. Do not dance to the tune of their negativity and impossibility. Like Joseph, nourish them and their children. Tell the people who despised you and sold you out that God has changed your story and given you honor for your shame, therefore, you do not hold anything against them. Give them a sense of assurance that your good intentions for them are genuine. Let them know that you do not have an ulterior motive. Your yes is your yes and you are determined to bless them because God has blessed you.

Over the years, I have come to totally believe in the truth that God will bless you in order for you to become a blessing. God is not a covenant breaker and His words are yes and amen. God will definitely bless you but the onus lies on you to extend that blessing to others. In fact, the Bible posits that: *There is that scattereth, and yet increaseth; and there is that withholdeth more than is meet, but it tendeth to poverty* (Proverbs 11:24, NLT). See how the New Living Translation (NLT) renders the same scripture: *Give freely and become more wealthy; be stingy and lose everything.* God has blessed you beyond your wildest imagination and you can give back His glory to Him by being a blessing to others; even to the people who despised you.

Further, give God praise for the daily provisions and blessings. When you have eaten and you are full, God cautions one to give Him the praise due His name. Keep dancing and keep giving God all the praise; even when no one understands you and the world calls you names. It will be well with you and you will live a long and a meaningful life.

Backmatter

About The Author

Dr. Pastor. Mrs. Priscilla Naamomo Otubuah is the First Lady of Victory Bible Church International, Living Waters Sanctuary City (Ontario, California). She serves as the president of the women's ministry, leader of the teaching ministry (school of the Word), supervising minister of the music ministry and overseer of the health ministry (Victory Health Ministry). Priscilla holds a double doctorate degree in nursing (Doctor of Philosophy, PhD; and Doctor of Nursing Practice, DNP). She is also a dually board-certified Family Nurse Practitioner and a Psychiatric Mental Health Nurse Practitioner. Priscilla is the founder and president of MarketStyle International Health Outreach (MaSiHo), a non-for-profit organization focused on delivering healthcare in a market style to the nations of the world. She is married to Rev. Akrofi Otubuah and they are blessed with a son,

Nii Kunim Kabu Otubuah. Priscilla is the author of the following books: *Service, Your Access to Royalty* and *Lord, Please Speak to the Fish*.

CPSIA information can be obtained
at www.ICGtesting.com
Printed in the USA
LVHW011205190522
719134LV00012B/288